Morina
TO

Jax
FROM

July 2010
DATE

# Home Spa Escapes

ARTWORK BY

Kathy
Hatch

HARVEST HOUSE PUBLISHERS

EUGENE, OREGON

# Home Spa Escapes

Text Copyright © 2009 by Harvest House Publishers
Published by Harvest House Publishers
Eugene, Oregon 97402
www.harvesthousepublishers.com

ISBN 978-0-7369-2303-3

Artwork © by Kathy Hatch and used by Harvest House Publishers, Inc. under authorization from MHS Licensing, Minneapolis, Minnesota. For more information regarding art prints featured in this book, please contact:

MHS Licensing
11100 Wayzata Blvd., Suite 550
Minneapolis, MN 55305
(952) 544-1377
www.mhslicensing.com

Design and production by Koechel Peterson & Associates, Inc., Minneapolis, Minnesota

Scripture quotations are taken from the HOLY BIBLE, NEW INTERNATIONAL VERSION®. NIV®. Copyright©1973, 1978, 1984 by the International Bible Society. Used by permission of Zondervan. All rights reserved.

Harvest House Publishers has made every effort to trace the ownership of all poems and quotes. In the event of a question arising from the use of a poem or quote, we regret any error made and will be pleased to make the necessary correction in future editions of this book.

**Printed in China**

09 10 11 12 13 14 15 / LP / 10 9 8 7 6 5 4 3 2 1

*W*hy add the stress of high-priced spa appointments to your life? Pampering can take place anytime when you transform your home into your favorite luxury spa. Relax in the warmth of inspirational thoughts as you try these simple and effective treatments to restore shine to your hair, radiance to your skin, and energy to tired muscles.

This little book is your big invitation to escape life's demands and embrace life's delights—rest your mind, nourish your body, and uplift your soul.

*Take rest; a field that has rested gives a bountiful crop.*

* OVID *

# The contemplative life

must provide an area, a space
of *liberty,* of silence,
in which possibilities are allowed
to surface and *new choices*—
beyond routine choice—
*become* manifest.

*Thomas Merton*

Reason's whole pleasure,
all the joys of sense,
Lie in three words:
health, peace,
and competence.

ALEXANDER POPE

Perfume and incense
bring joy to the heart.

The Book of Proverbs

You can't do anything
about the length of your life,
but you can do something
about its width and depth.

* EVAN ESAR *

# Herbal Hair Rinse

## FOR SOFT, SHINY, HEALTHY HAIR

### INGREDIENTS

2 tablespoons dried herb of choice

or

4 tablespoons fresh herb

4 cups boiling water

1 tablespoon vinegar

Large glass pitcher

Strainer

### INSTRUCTIONS

Place herb of choice in pitcher. Pour boiling water over the herb. Let steep for 10 to 15 minutes. Strain out the herb. Add 1 tablespoon vinegar.

Pour warm rinse over hair after shampooing and conditioning. Do not rinse.

# For Strong & Beautiful
# HAIR

───∞ INSTRUCTIONS ∞───

Mix 2 egg yolks with 2 teaspoons
castor oil. Massage mixture into hair for 5-6 minutes.
Rinse thoroughly.

*Beauty as we feel it
is something indescribable.
What it is or what it means
can never be said.*

George Santayana

# summer strands makeover

Give your hair a summer shine makeover
in every season of the year. Mix together
½ cup apple cider vinegar and ½ cup water
in a spray bottle. Shake gently. Spray your hair
thoroughly with the mixture. After a few minutes,
rinse hair with cool water.

*One's destination*

is never a place but

rather a new way

of *looking*

at things.

**Henry Miller**

# HOMEMADE HERBAL
## Shampoo

### INGREDIENTS

4 ounces castile soap
½ ounce rosemary
½ ounce sage
½ ounce lavender

### INSTRUCTIONS

Mix all ingredients together.
Store in bottle.

*There is no pleasure in having nothing to do;*
*the fun is having lots to do—and not doing it.*

\* MARY WILSON LITTLE \*

Sit in reverie,
and watch the changing
color of the waves that
break upon the idle
seashore of the mind.

HENRY WADSWORTH LONGFELLOW

herbal
hair
treat

# Dry Hair Treatment

## INGREDIENTS

Mix together
½ cup honey
¼ cup olive oil
(2 tablespoons for normal/oily hair)

## INSTRUCTIONS

Using a small amount at a time,
work mixture through hair
until coated. Cover hair with
shower cap and leave on
for 30 minutes.

Remove cap, shampoo well, and rinse.

To sit in the shade on a fine day and look upon verdure is the most perfect refreshment.

JANE AUSTEN

Taking joy in life is a woman's best cosmetic.

Rosalind Russell

# FIRMING
# Facial Mask

~~~ INGREDIENTS ~~~

Whisk together
1 tablespoon honey
1 egg white
1 teaspoon glycerin *(available at drug stores)*
1-2 tablespoons flour *(enough to form paste)*

~~~ INSTRUCTIONS ~~~

Smooth over face and throat.
Leave on 10 minutes and wash off
with warm water. Pat dry.

*sweet*

Besides the *noble* art of getting things done, there is a nobler *art* of leaving things undone. The *wisdom* of life consists in the elimination of *nonessentials*.

*Lin Yutang*

What *sweet delight* a quiet life affords.

* WILLIAM DRUMMOND *

# a HOMEGROWN HONEY-GLOW FACIAL

Pick up some local honey
at a farmer's market or local organic store.
Select unprocessed honey only. Not only will it add
flavor to your toast in the morning, but this fresh honey
will also add a glow to your face. Secure your hair away
from your face and then apply a thin layer of honey
on your face and neck. Relax for 10 to 15 minutes
and then rinse the honey off with warm water.

*Drink in life and savor every drop—
the sweet and the sour, the good and
the bad, the planned and the unplanned.
When you do, you'll feel fully alive.*

Luci Swindoll

We need to find God, and he cannot be found in noise and restlessness. God is the friend of silence. See how nature—trees, flowers, grass—grows in silence; see the stars, the moon and the sun, how they move in silence... We need silence to be able to touch souls.

MOTHER TERESA

*Leisure,* the highest happiness upon earth, is seldom enjoyed with perfect *satisfaction,* except in solitude.

Johann Georg von Zimmermann

*Beauty is the gift of God.*

\* ARISTOTLE \*

# Pampered Face
# EXFOLIANT

1 teaspoon ground oatmeal
1 teaspoon ground cornmeal
1 teaspoon honey
1 teaspoon plain yogurt
2 tablespoons chamomile tea
*(For a fragrant option, add 2 drops lavender essential oil)*

Mix the ingredients together until they have
the consistency of a paste. Apply to the face gently.
Rub into the skin and then rinse off.
Gently pat skin dry.

Without respite

the human condition would overwhelm;

without comedy and laughter

there would be too much

seriousness and grim resolve.

* LEWIS RICHARD *

I loaf and invite my soul.

Walt Whitman

# Citrus Refresher

## INGREDIENTS

7 ounces plain yogurt
1 tablespoon lemon juice
1 tablespoon honey

## INSTRUCTIONS

Blend ingredients, massage into skin,
and then rinse off. The lemon juice will
help exfoliate dead skin cells, and
the yogurt and honey will calm and
refresh your skin. Be prepared to glow.

A cheerful look
brings joy
to the heart,
and good news
gives health
to the bones.

* THE BOOK OF PROVERBS *

It would be also of great use to us to form our deliberate judgments in persons and things in the calmest and serenest hours of life, when the passions of nature are all silent, and the mind enjoys its most perfect composure.

ISAAC WATTS

# BROWN SUGAR CITRUS
# Body Scrub

## INGREDIENTS

⅔ cup brown sugar
⅓ cup almond oil
½ teaspoon vitamin E
20 drops vanilla essential oil
15 drops lemon essential oil
10 drops orange essential oil

## INSTRUCTIONS

Mix thoroughly and store in airtight container.

There is one piece
of advice, in a life of study,
which I think no one will object to;
and that is, every now and then,
to be completely idle—
to do nothing at all.

Sydney Smith

*Happiness depends on a leisurely breakfast.*

* JOHN GUNTHER *

*Silence*

is the secret

to *sanity.*

Astrid Alauda

# Banana Beautiful

INGREDIENTS

1 ripe banana
3 to 4 tablespoons coarse sugar

INSTRUCTIONS

Using a fork, blend ingredients
together into a paste.
Then rub this combination
on your legs in gentle, circular motions.
Rinse off and feel
the appeal of
banana beauty.

# smooth out the rough places
# Sugar Scrub

## INGREDIENTS

*½ cup cane sugar (coarse sugar is best)*
*½ cup olive or sesame oil*
*1 drop peppermint essential oil*

## INSTRUCTIONS

Mix ingredients. Feel free to increase the
amounts in order to have more scrub to use.
Rub this mixture into your skin. Focus on any
rough spots or trouble areas, such as your elbows
and heels, and then gently rub all over for
an invigorating and enjoyable scrub.

Love the moment, and the
energy of that moment will spread
beyond all boundaries.
* CORITA KENT *

Life is short, and
it's up to you to make it sweet.
Sadie Delany

Look to this day!

For it is life, the very life of life.

For yesterday is but a dream

And tomorrow is only a vision

But today well lived makes every

yesterday a dream of happiness

And tomorrow a vision of hope.

Look well, therefore, to this day!

Such is the salutation of the dawn.

KALIDASA

# Aches to Ahhhs
## ESSENTIAL OIL RECIPE

### ～ INGREDIENTS ～

*3 drops peppermint oil*
*3 drops lemongrass oil*
*3 drops basil oil*

*Do not Disturb*

### ～ INSTRUCTIONS ～

Mix these oils together and rub into
sore muscles or painful joints. If the mixture
feels too warm or your skin is sensitive,
dilute with a bit of your favorite base oil.
This combination will relieve pain
and ease your aches.

# LAVENDER
## Body Salt Scrub

### ~ INGREDIENTS ~

2 cups Epsom salts
1/2 cup sea salt
6 drops lavender essential oil
2 teaspoons dried lavender

### ~ INSTRUCTIONS ~

Mix all ingredients together
and store in sealed jar.

*Cheerfulness* keeps
up a kind of *daylight*
in the *mind*, filling it
with a steady and
perpetual *serenity*.

Joseph Addison

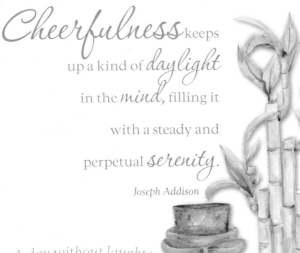

*A day without laughter
is a day wasted.*
* CHARLIE CHAPLIN *

The heart that is to be filled to the brim with holy joy must be held still.

George Seaton Bowes

What sunshine is to flowers, smiles are to humanity.

These are but trifles, to be sure;

but scattered along life's pathway,

the good they do is inconceivable.

* JOSEPH ADDISON *

Happiness
is like a butterfly
which, when pursued,
is always beyond our grasp,
but, if you will sit down quietly,
may alight upon you.

NATHANIEL HAWTHORNE

dreamy
cream

10 oz

Climb the mountains

and get their good tidings.

Nature's peace will flow into you

as sunshine flows into trees.

The winds will blow

their own freshness into you,

and the storms their energy,

while cares will drop away

from you like the leaves of Autumn.

\* JOHN MUIR \*

# Georgia's Butter Dream
# LOTION

INGREDIENTS

¼ cup grated cocoa butter

1 tablespoon coconut oil

3 tablespoons sunflower oil

11 tablespoons grated beeswax

## INSTRUCTIONS

Combine all ingredients in a glass container
and melt in the microwave. Be careful that the
mixture doesn't boil. Stir well and continue stirring
regularly while the mixture cools completely.
Put into a jar or jars with lids
when completely cooled.

To have someone who brings out the colors of life and whose very presence offers tranquility and contentment enriches my being and makes me grateful for the opportunity to share.

KATHLEEN TIERNEY CRILLY

# Fresh Foot Soak

## INGREDIENTS

3 tablespoons baking soda
2 drops lemon essential oil

## INSTRUCTIONS

Dissolve the baking soda in a basin
of warm water for a lovely way
to relax your feet. Add 1 to 2 drops
lemon essential oil for added
invigoration. This is a great summertime
treat to keep feet clean and fresh
feeling and smelling.

All mankind's troubles are caused
by one single thing,
which is their inability to sit
quietly in a room.

* PASCAL *

It is the nature
of a great mind to be calm
and undisturbed.

Seneca

# the art of the bath

For the perfect relaxing bath, first set the mood.
Fill the tub with 95–100-degree water. Dim the lights
and surround yourself with scented candles.
Put on your favorite music. Allow your tub to fill,
and then add relaxing aromatherapy bubble bath or
bath oil. Immerse yourself, sit back, close your eyes,
quiet your mind, and relax....

# Relaxation
# & Stress Relief
# Bath Oil

## INGREDIENTS

1 ounce sweet almond oil
3 drops lavender essential oil
3 drops tangerine essential oil
3 drops marjoram essential oil
1 drop chamomile essential oil

## INSTRUCTIONS

Add to your bath water to help induce
deep relaxation of the tissues, muscles,
and joints and reestablish
a good Energy Balance.

*If it is a woman's nature to nurture,*

*then she must nourish herself.*

\* ANNE MORROW LINDBERG \*

I can't think of any
sorrow in the world
that a hot bath
wouldn't help just
a little bit.

SUSAN GLASPELL

*Take* all the *pleasures* of all the spheres,

And *multiply* each through endless years,

One minute of Heaven is *worth* them all.

Thomas Moore

*rest*

Know how to do good
a little at a time,
and often.

* BALTASAR GRACIAN *

My Favorite Songs

My
Journal

A world
without a Sabbath
would be like a man
without a smile,
like a summer
without flowers, and
like a homestead
without a garden.

Henry Ward Beecher

# Sea Sanctuary
# SOAK

*Calm dry skin and de-stress your day
with this easy yet luxurious soak.*

## INGREDIENTS

1 cup Epsom salts
1 cup sea salt
1 cup sesame oil

## INSTRUCTIONS

Add these ingredients to a warm tub of water
and indulge in a peaceful, soothing time.

The time to *relax* is when you don't have time for it.

* SYDNEY J. HARRIS *

# SOFT AS SILK

Savor an inexpensive and quick spa experience
anytime by adding either ¼ cup baking soda
or ½ cup powdered milk to your bath.
Your skin will be silky smooth and look as though
you spent a day at the spa!

# Sweet Dreams

*When you want a good night's sleep that leaves you refreshed in the morning, try this simple bath sachet.*

## INGREDIENTS

Dried chamomile flowers
Dried lavender buds
Dried rose petals

## INSTRUCTIONS

Combine these floral delights
and then place a couple of handfuls
of this mixture into a nylon, tied at both ends
to secure them. Then attach it to the spout
in your bathtub and have the water pour
through the bag, or simply swish the bag
around in the water.
Your bath and your evening will be infused
with gentle, serene aromas.

The best and most beautiful things in the world cannot be seen, nor touched... but are felt in the heart.

HELEN KELLER

*Cherish* all your happy *moments*. They make a *fine* cushion for old age.

*Christopher Morely*

Since you are like
no other being ever created
since the beginning of time,
you are incomparable.

*Brenda Ueland*

Happiness is found in doing,
not merely possessing.

\* NAPOLEON HILL \*

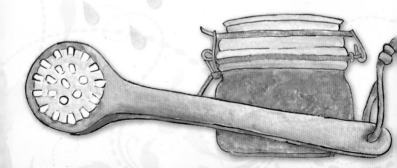

*True silence* is the *rest* of the mind; it is to the *spirit* what sleep is to the body, *nourishment* and refreshment.

William Penn

# NO TIME FOR A RELAXING BATH?
## INDULDGE IN A
## *Pampering Shower*

Just because you don't have time for a long
hot bath doesn't mean you shouldn't be able
to pamper yourself in the shower.

### KEEP YOUR SHOWER STOCKED WITH
*Your favorite aromatherapy shower gel*
*sea salt body scrub*
*invigorating massage brush*

Dry off with a soft fluffy
towel and pamper your skin
by applying a moisturizing
body lotion all over.
Wrap up in your favorite robe.

# SCENTED
## Shower Gel

~~~~~~ INGREDIENTS ~~~~~~

1 cup  unscented shampoo
½ cup water
1 ½ tablespoons salt
12–15 drops of fragrance oil
food coloring (optional)

~~~~~~ INSTRUCTIONS ~~~~~~

Use fragrance oil of your choice
to achieve the desired aromatherapy effect.

# *Cherish* your own *emotions* and never undervalue them.

Robert Henri

* *Lavender for Stress Relief*
* *Lemon to Energize*
* *Chamomile for Meditation*
* *Rose for Romance*

Ocean Breeze shower gel

8 oz

Let's awaken our hearts, minds, and spirits so that we don't waste the sacred gift of a day. Even a regular day has its miracle moments.

HOPE LYDA

Look up, laugh, love, and live.

Mary Martin

# PET SPA

All seasons are beautiful
for the person who carries
happiness within.

* HORACE FRIESS *

*Tension* is who you think you should be.

*Relaxation* is who you are.

Chinese Proverb

# Herbal Dog Shampoo

*Dogs like to be pampered too…*

 **INGREDIENTS**

¹/₃ cup glycerin

1 cup all natural dish soap

1 cup apple cider vinegar

1 quart water

*few drops each of:*

tea tree oil

lavender oil

citronella oil

**INSTRUCTIONS**

Mix all ingredients into a large bottle, shake well, and use as needed. Rinse dog well after each bath.

# Natural Aromatic
# SPRAY

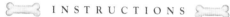 INSTRUCTIONS

Pour the following essential oils
into a 1-ounce spray bottle filled with water:

*10 drops lavender*
*10 drops geranuim*
*6 drops lemon*

Shake vigorously
several times before
each use. Spray directly
onto your dog, holding
bottle about 10" away.
Avoid spraying on head
and near eyes.

Be it mine
to draw from wisdom's fount,
pure as it flows, that calm
of soul which virtue
only knows.

Aeschylus

Enjoy your own life
without comparing it to another.

* MARQUIS DE CONDORCET *

Every good thought you think

is contributing its share

to the ultimate result of your life.

* GRENVILLE KLEISER *

Keep yourself alive
by throwing day by day
fresh currents of thought
and emotion into the
things you have come
to do from habit.

JOHN LANCASTER SPALDING

Sometimes
the most urgent thing
you can possibly do
is take a complete rest.

Ashleigh Brilliant